A Rookie reader®

I Need a Little Help

Written by Kathy Schulz
Illustrated by Ann Iosa

Children's Press®
A Division of Scholastic Inc.
New York • Toronto • London • Auckland • Sydney
Mexico City • New Delhi • Hong Kong
Danbury, Connecticut

To my parents for helping us out when Baxter needed a little help
—K.S.

To Michael John Iosa
—A.I.

Reading Consultants

Linda Cornwell
Literacy Specialist

Katharine A. Kane
Education Consultant
(Retired, San Diego County Office of Education and San Diego State University)

Library of Congress Cataloging-in-Publication Data

Schulz, Kathy.
  I need a little help / written by Kathy Schulz ; illustrated by Ann
Iosa.- 1st American ed.
       p. cm. — (Rookie reader)
Summary: After a young boy asks for help in doing various things
throughout the day, he expresses his gratitude to those who came to his aid.
  ISBN 0-516-22877-3 (lib. bdg.)   0-516-27833-9 (pbk.)
  [1. Life skills—Fiction. 2. Self-reliance—Fiction. 3. Gratitude—Fiction.
4. Stories in rhyme.] I. Iosa, Ann, ill. II. Title.
III. Series.
  PZ8.3.S2974Iae 2003
  [E]—dc21
                                          2003003884

CHILDREN'S PRESS, and A ROOKIE READER®, and associated logos are
trademarks and or registered trademarks of Scholastic Library Publishing.
SCHOLASTIC and associated logos are trademarks and or registered trademarks
of Scholastic Inc.
9 10 R 12 11 10 09   62

I need a little help.

Will you help me tie my shoes?

I need a little help.

Will you help me read the news?

I need a little help.

Will you help me fix my boat?

I need a little help.

Will you help me zip my coat?

I need a little help.

Will you help me find a seat?

Thank you for your help.
Will you help me share my treat?

Word List (25 words)

a	for	my	share	treat
boat	help	need	shoes	will
coat	I	news	thank	you
find	little	read	the	your
fix	me	seat	tie	zip

About the Author

Kathy Schulz has written two other books in the A Rookie Reader® series — **Get Out of My Chair** and **Always Be Safe**. She has enjoyed sharing the process of publishing her books with her first grade students, and she likes hearing their ideas about what her next book should be. Kathy also enjoys being a volunteer at a local animal shelter, where she spends many hours walking and cuddling dogs and puppies.

About the Illustrator

Ann Iosa lives in a small town in Connecticut with her husband and two children. She graduated from Paier School of Art in Connecticut and has illustrated many wonderful children's books.